Love, Nurture, and Forgive

Love, Nurture, and Forgive

A Handbook to Add a New Richness to Your Life

Ryuho Okawa

Lantern Books • New York
A Division of Booklight Inc.

Lantern Books
One Union Square West, Suite 2001
New York, NY 10003

English Translation © 2002
Translated by The Institute for Research
in Human Happiness, Ltd.
Original title: "Hito-o-Aishi, Hito-o-Ikashi, Hito-o-Yuruse"

Library of Congress Cataloging-in-Publication Data

Okawa, Ryuho, 1956-
[Hito o aishi, hito o ikashi, hito o yuruse. English]
Love, nurture, and forgive : a handbook to add a new richness to your life / Ryuho Okawa.
    p. cm.
ISBN 1-930051-78-6 (alk. paper)
1. Kofuku no Kagaku (Organization) 2. Spiritual life. I. Title.

BP605.K55 O32413 2002
299'.93—dc21
                                    2002000659

Table of Contents

Introduction

This book presents a philosophy of life, or rather, it is a hand-book for a philosophy of life. The words of this title, "Love, Nurture, and Forgive," although only a phrase, brought about a major transformation in my life. To be more precise, it was when I understood the true meaning of these words that I attained enlightenment. This occurred back in 1981.

In the twenty years that have passed since then, the organization that I created to carry out the aims inherent in this phrase, "Love, Nurture, and Forgive," the Institute for Research in Human Happiness, has grown to become one of the largest spiritual movements in Japan. One small phrase of Truth has grown remarkably and now bears fruits in such abundance.

I am delighted to have so many outstanding men and women as the members of IRH. When I think about what makes these people outstanding, I find that the secret lies in their attitude of self-help, being willing to take responsibility for improving themselves. People who devote themselves to self-improvement and the practice of altruism, as described in this book, will develop day by day. Within six months to a year, they will succeed in transforming themselves to become completely different people.

All through this book are words of light that are essential for all who wish to live a rich life. I have no doubt whatsoever that you will find this a useful handbook to help you throughout your life.

I strongly hope that, with the key phrase "Love, Nurture, and Forgive" always in mind, all who read this book will develop a richer life by practicing "love that gives."

Ryuho Okawa
January 2002

Part One

Love, Nurture, and Forgive

I. How the "Stages of Love" Philosophy Started

1. The Core Words of the Philosophy

The phrase, "Love, Nurture, and Forgive" is very dear to me, and it fills me with courage. When I look back over past years and remember where I started out, these words always come to mind.

It all began back in 1981. In those days I was living a completely different lifestyle and never imagined that the time would come when it would be my job to teach spiritual truths. One day, however, I suddenly started to receive messages from another dimension, from a world that exists beyond this world on Earth. It was a totally unexpected reality that opened up before me, without any warning.

In the following years, I read widely on spirituality and realized that there were others who had had similar experiences. One was Mother Teresa of Calcutta, who one day heard the voice of Jesus Christ when she was traveling on a train, and realized her life's mission. After that she began her great work in India.

At the time, although I did not doubt that such extraordinary phenomena could occur to others, I had absolutely no idea how to cope when they happened to me personally. Being totally unprepared, I was astounded by my first spiritual revelation. It happened in this way.

In the afternoon of March 23, 1981, I had a premonition that something special was about to happen. I picked up an index card and waited, pencil in hand. Suddenly my hand began to move as if it had a life of its own. It was quite obvious that I was not moving it. To start with, it wrote the Japanese characters meaning "Good News" on the first sheet of card.

On the second sheet, the message "Good News" was written, and on the third sheet, too. My hand continued to do this over and over again on new cards, until finally I said, "I know that, but don't you have something else to tell me?" However, my hand just continued to write "Good News." That was all that happened that day, but I had a strong sense of anticipation that something more was going to follow.

Although I did not know how to react to this kind of spiritual communication, I soon became quite used to it and started to have conversations with beings who were not of this world. One of the messages that I received at this time was "Love, Nurture, and Forgive." Based on the ideas expressed in this phrase, I was later to develop my philosophy of the developmental stages of love.

I considered the meaning of this simple message for several months until finally I understood that it summed up the core of the philosophy I was to develop and what was to become my life's work in this world. I continued to ponder this single line of text for almost three years in total. During this period, I experienced numerous spiritual phenomena but I remained an employee of a major Japanese trading company, repeating the words to myself as I tried to discover some way I could put them into practice. Finally, when I was about twenty-seven years old, I managed to develop these simple words into the "Stages of Love" philosophy.[1] Three years of contemplation had convinced me that there were different developmental stages of love.

As I look back, I can say that when this philosophy took a clear shape it marked the beginning of the next phase of my own spiritual development. It took me three years to develop the philosophy of the "Stages of Love," and then it was a further three years before I felt ready to go out and actually teach spiritual truths publicly. During those six years I contemplated how to develop my philosophy based on this key phrase and put it into actual practice.

2. Love that Gives

As I continued to reflect upon this phrase, I gradually came to realize that the three factors—loving, nurturing, and forgiving—all indicated a certain direction. To love people, to nurture them, and to forgive them all represented a positive approach toward relationships, without thinking of any return for oneself. In other words, they represented a form of altruism.

However, at the time when I received the key phrase in 1981, I was only twenty-four years old and my natural tendencies were quite the opposite. *I* wanted to be loved, nurtured, and forgiven. All I desired was that other people love me, were kind to me, and praised me. I longed to hear people say how much they admired me, I needed it so badly it hurt. However, these three words urged me to make a complete, one-hundred-and-eighty-degree change of perspective.

---

1. Refer to Chapter 3, "The River of Love," in *The Laws of the Sun*, by Ryuho Okawa, Lantern Books (2001).

I must admit, I did ask myself what I could possibly hope to gain from doing this. On the other hand, I saw so much evil and contradiction in the world that I did not know where to begin forgiving. I was filled with moral indignation; I could not find it within me to forgive the world as it was, and felt an overwhelming desire to judge it. However, from about six months before I came into contact with the phrase, "Love, Nurture, and Forgive," I began to have plenty of opportunities to look back over my life. Faced with difficulties and worries, I became very introspective.

At that time, there were two preoccupations that troubled me most. The first was related to the realization of my personal goals. I felt very strongly that I wanted to develop my abilities fully and live the kind of life I felt I deserved. I had a very powerful desire to live my ideals, but things did not always turn out as I would have liked them to. As a result, I suffered a lot of disappointment, and felt as if an irrational force was placing blocks in the road ahead of me.

The other problem was to do with love. It is only natural for human beings to want to be loved by others. In this, everybody is the same and we very often suffer, particularly in adolescence, because we are unable to receive love. If I were to analyze my feelings at this time, I would have to admit that, contrary to what I teach at IRH now, I paid very little regard to everything people had done for me. On the other hand, when I was unable to attain the goals I desired or get people to do things my way, I became frustrated, disappointed, and unhappy. What is more, I felt that this way of living was quite normal.

I like poetry, and from about the age of ten I started to write a large number of poems. I think this indicates that I was one of those people who tend to be very sensitive and prone to negativity, who is easily hurt and vents their feelings of hurt by writing poems. While I was incapable of feeling immediate joy when I received praise, the slightest insult would pierce me like a thorn and rankle me for years.

People say all kinds of things in different circumstances, and in many cases they do not intend to hurt others. If this applies to you, then it applies to others. It is that simple. Unfortunately, however, some people are incapable of thinking in this way, and I was one of them. When somebody made a careless remark to me, without any particular intention to hurt, just voicing a thought that had popped into their head, they probably did not think any more of it. However, this kind of carelessness would stab me, like a dagger in the heart, and sometimes the hurt remained for years. This resulted in my suffering an immense sense of frustration; I thought I was the most pitiful of all human beings. I felt I was worthless and could not understand why I had been born at all.

When faced with the ideas contained in the phrase, "Love, Nurture, and Forgive," I came to the realization that perhaps the happiness I had been pursuing all these years was not real happiness after all. Up until that time, I had thought that happiness was something to be bestowed by others. I was happy if I received the praise and admiration from others I felt I deserved. However, there was absolutely no hint of "receiving" in the key phrase.

I looked back over my life and asked myself if I had ever actually loved anybody, or whether I had even tried to love others, but I could think of very few instances of having done so. To the contrary, the more I thought about it, the more I realized how much others had done for me over the years. First of all, my parents had never stinted themselves to do their best for me. I also recognized just how much I owed my friends and teachers for all they had done to help me in my life. It was their support and the environment they had created which had enabled me to devote myself to my studies. However, I had only thought of myself; I had only thought of the happiness my own achievement and success would bring me.

Then I tried to make a mental list of everything that people had done for me and everything I had done for others—this is a practical technique I now refer to as the "Love Balance Sheet." The result was that, no matter how hard I tried, I could think of very few occasions when I had done anything for others, or when I had made an effort to try and make somebody else happy. On the other hand, I could come up with any number of situations where somebody else had gone out of their way in order to help me. Things that I had done for others, things that were genuinely good, went into the "assets" column whereas things that others had done to help me went into the "liabilities" column. When I added them all up, I deeply regretted the way I had been living and knew I needed to become a new person.

I had never looked at the world in this light before. In the past, I had been quite satisfied if, say, I achieved good results in a test and had been praised for it. I would feel I had achieved something important. I had considered that as long as I was the center of attention it meant I was leading a perfect life. However, once I was able to change my perspective, I realized what a terrible life I had been living up until that time.

3. False Love

I looked at the world from a completely new angle. I thought: "There are over five billion people living on the Earth and over one hundred million in Japan alone. If all these people were to list the things they had done for others in one column and the things that others had done for them in the other, in the same way that I did, what would the results be? If most of them had had things done for them without doing anything in return, then it would mean that the majority of the people on this planet were debtors, living like spiritual parasites on the love stolen from others."

If you go into a rice field or marsh, slimy leeches may fasten themselves to your legs and suck your blood. Everybody finds them obnoxious, for the reason that leeches steal people's blood instead of doing anything productive. The same is true of mosquitoes. We hate the way they materialize invisibly and steal our blood before making off again. Many people actually act in exactly the same way. They do not produce anything useful, but walk off with what others have expended a lot of effort to create.

People who are always complaining that nobody loves them, nobody ever gives them any praise or admiration, that they are never able to achieve their potential—people who feel it is their due to be loved and who offer nothing in return—can be compared to leeches or mosquitoes. It is only natural that these sorts of people are disliked.

It is hard to imagine that someone would purposely go to a place where there are a lot of mosquitoes, roll up their sleeves, and gladly offer them as much blood as they want. Like mosquitoes, people who only ever think of what they can take from others will naturally not be liked, or at the very least, they will not get what they ask for.

This can occur in relationships between men and women. Particularly in adolescence, young people crave the love of the opposite sex. If they do not get it, it is the cause of endless worry, but do they ever consider what they could give? If they do happen to do things for a partner, is it not usually because they expect something in return? Although people may think they are practicing "love that gives," many are actually only doing something because they expect some kind of reward. If they do not receive anything in return, their love will be transformed to become a source of pain because it was not true to begin with. Love that expects something in return is not true love.

If somebody were to give you a Christmas present simply because they wanted something in return, you would not be impressed. People give presents to express their goodwill and gratitude. Although they may well receive something in return, there is something wrong with people whose only motivation in giving is to get something back. This is very easy to understand when we talk about presents, but people do the same on the spiritual plane; they tend to expect something in return.

Please reflect on yourself and try to compare what you have done for others with what has been done for you. If the two balance, then you are not in debt and deserve to be called a good human being. However, if more things have been done for you than you have done in return, that means you have been a burden on people around you. In other words, you are living your life in debt.

4. Self-Development Through the "Love that Gives"

It is surprising to learn just how much we receive from others and how little we do for them in return. When I was faced with this truth, I began to think there must be a happiness that was far greater than the happiness I thought I could achieve if some of my wishes came true.

We experience happiness when our sense of our own being is strong, and our sense of being grows when we feel we have grown. The wish to be recognized and appreciated must come from the desire to grow, but this desire cannot be fulfilled by taking love from others. That is merely an attempt to fill in the parts of ourselves we feel are missing.

Self-development in a truest sense is planting a part of your own soul, spirit, mind, or heart in others. It is important that your way of living or thinking has a positive influence on others. We generally think that to give is to lose while to receive is to gain. But in the spiritual realm the more we give the more we grow. For instance, in my case, to be able to stand in front of tens of thousands of people and give a talk is a form of personal development. I am able to influence the thinking of each person in the audience and add something to their lives. This is much more meaningful than adding something to my own life, and it results in much greater self-development.

Therefore, the true path to self-development does not lie in defending one's own interests. The satisfaction this sort of attempt brings is actually very small. True happiness can be found in the understanding that you are infinitely good and useful to others. So, if you wish to experience growth and development, you should try to help as many people as possible. This is egoism in the best sense of the word. Most people remain satisfied with small feelings of contentment, but all those years ago I realized that if you really want to do good for yourself, then you must completely change your perspective on life.

II. What It Means to Love Others

1. The "Love that Gives" Can Change Your Life

It is easy to say that it is important to love others, but much harder to put this into practice. What comes to mind when people ask you what it means to love others in everyday life? Do you think it simply means to offer others your seat in a crowded train or pick up a small child who has fallen over? This is a very difficult question to answer and, unfortunately, nobody has ever written a book that lists exactly what it means to love others. It is something you have to discover for yourself.

If you are married, you may believe that you love your spouse so much that you have devoted all your love to him or her. However, in this case, are you sure that what you think of as love is the same love I am talking about? Do you not assume that just because you have devoted yourself to your partner it is only natural that you should receive something in return? Do you not think you are practicing "the love that gives" when in fact you are really trying to bind your spouse closer to you? Are you not limiting your partner's activities or thoughts in the name of love? When seen from this viewpoint, can you really say that your love is not in some way mistaken? This is something you have no way of seeing until questioned by others.

The same is true of a parent's love for a child. People may think they love their children when in actual fact all this means is that they are just in a habit of constantly worrying. They worry that their child is going to be involved in a traffic accident, will fail exams, or will fall in with a bad crowd. This is all they can think of and in this way they confuse worry with love. Although they think they are worrying for their children, in actual fact the parents are worrying for their own sake. Their real worry is what will happen to them if their worst fears come true.

For instance, a parent whose child is due to take the entrance examinations for university may worry about what will happen if their child fails. But are they really thinking about their child's future? I think that in many cases they are more worried about what other people will say or the fact they will have to go through the bother of preparing for the exams again for one more year.

In this way, when you reflect on yourself and check whether you have been giving your love purely for the sake of the other person, you will discover that it is not at all easy to practice "love that gives," the most basic teaching we study at IRH. In fact, it is extremely difficult to carry out, and is not something that can be accomplished without effort.

Then what should you do? You must first start with knowing that to give love is one of the most important objectives of your spiritual discipline and that by giving out loving thoughts, your whole life will start to change. I can assure you that this is absolutely true from my own experience. When I determined to stop craving praise, respect, and love from others, and instead started to do something that would help as many people as possible and make them happy, my life started to change.

Once I had made up my mind that I no longer desired the praise of others, that I did not want their gratitude but that I would simply devote my life to other people's well-being, I found things around me began to change as I progressed toward my goal. Numerous people appeared who agreed with what I was doing and who wanted to help me accomplish my aim. Nobody will offer to help if you only live for your own sake, but as soon as you decide to work for others, people will come to help you. This may sound mysterious, but it is a spiritual law.

2. Love Will Come to the One Who Gives It

In my books I have often said that "love that gives" is a love that expects nothing in return, and as soon as you expect something in return, love dies. When I say "as soon as you expect something in return, love dies," I do not do so to be poetic or because I think the words have a nice ring to them. I say it because it is the truth. If you do something good and then expect the equivalent or something even greater in return, the benefit achieved by the original act is canceled out.

The reason I say that you should expect nothing in return is that if something has been freely given, love will eventually return to the giver. This is one of the most important spiritual laws and it applies to each and every person. If nothing else, it is important that you become aware of this law while you are living on Earth. The love you have given will eventually come back to you—this is the law in the world that cannot be seen.

Many of you have probably read about the lives of great people, but have you ever paused to ask what made these people great? It was because they were willing to give endlessly without expecting anything in return. As a result, what they gave out eventually came back to them and became theirs. This is in accordance with the physical laws of the spiritual world, and the amount of light those people possessed was increased by their loving acts.

When you do something purely for the sake of others, the minute the thought enters your mind and you perform the action, a halo appears around your head. This halo is something given to you by the heavenly world. Although it is invisible to the eyes of those on Earth, a spiritual light is definitely being emitted.

This can be proved by the fact that whenever you do something out of a pure intention to make others happy, you will find your whole body filled with warmth. Not only the recipient, but also you yourself will feel warm. Even though it may be in the middle of winter, you will find yourself flooded with a feeling of warmth, and this is proof of the fact that you are radiating light.

With spiritual sight, it is possible to see your own halo reflected in a mirror. If you think good thoughts, a halo will suddenly appear behind your head. If your thoughts are full of love for others, although you may think you are giving love, you are actually receiving it.

This is closely related to the reason why God created mankind in the first place. I teach that human beings are all children of God and this means that we carry within us the same nature as God. The nature of God consists of a multitude of elements. But the most significant element is "love that gives." This means that we can manifest our essential nature as children of God when we are giving love to others.

When we practice the "love that gives," we can recognize our true nature and, as if in proof of this, we are blessed with light and begin to glow. This light may disappear in a minute or two, but those who always hold positive and giving thoughts will find themselves surrounded with smiles and light. You may sometimes notice that when a certain person enters a room, the room suddenly brightens up. This is because such people are always thinking of ways in which to make those around them happy, so their haloes are very bright. If you always hold positive thoughts in your mind, those positive thoughts will provide you with a constant source of strength and embody themselves in physical phenomena.

3. Act Without Expectation of Reward

Buddhism teaches us the merit of offering alms, but why is this so important? It was not because monks wanted to satisfy their appetite. It was taught because the love that is inherent in the act of giving, the virtue that it contains, returns to the giver. This is why the significance of giving is taught.

Shakyamuni Buddha continually taught monks and nuns that even though they may look like beggars, they should hold their heads high when accepting offerings. He taught, "You are not beggars, you are actually giving. By providing people with an opportunity to offer alms, you are giving great love. You are teaching them what is most important for human beings. The Truth is taught not only through preaching, but also expressed in the natural actions that are a part of everyday life.

"In the simple act of holding out your begging bowl, without saying a word, you have to be able to guide lay believers toward Truth. You must teach them how purifying it feels to give offerings, how noble, and how happy they will feel as a result. You must not belittle yourselves just because you are on the receiving end. You are not begging, you are offering them a revelation, a chance to receive great light. You are presenting them with the means to achieve enlightenment. Remember that the collecting of alms is a discipline that leads to great enlightenment and practice this daily. It is also a way of teaching others and guiding them closer to the Truth."

What Shakyamuni taught was absolutely right, and there is an important point to remember from the standpoint of those who offer. If they place an offering of food or drink in a monk's bowl, expecting they will find salvation in the next world or their sins will be removed, then all merit that the action may have brought will be canceled out. What is given will eventually return to those who gave. But if the giver ever expects to be rewarded, the merit is negated and spiritually, he or she will never gain anything.

A large number of people have awakened to the Truth and are making a concerted effort to spread light; many of them are involved in various forms of volunteer work. I would like to say to them that an earnest desire to help others is of itself worthy of respect. When this is put into practice, it becomes a source of great merit to the one who is giving, as the love given out will return to them. You must never list all your good deeds, nor should you try to win recognition from others. You must try and forget all the acts of love you have performed and the love you have given others.

It does no good to list all the things you have done or try to remember them. Even worse is to expect to be treated in a special way for what you have done, or to expect something in return. If you do this, you will not be able to make any progress as a seeker of Truth. It can even be said you are actually moving in the opposite direction. Although you may have good thoughts and do good deeds, it is important you forget them afterward.

Good thoughts and good actions have to come naturally and spontaneously. You must move or talk naturally without forcing yourself. You must do so because you want to, because it gives you pleasure and you have enjoyed doing these things all your life. This kind of attitude is very important. You do not need to let others know what you do. If you try to advertise your good deeds, any merit they bring will be negated, so just try and forget what you have done.

On the other hand, although it is difficult, you need to make the effort to remember every time somebody else does something for you. It is easy for us to remember what we have done for others, and forget what others have done for us. This is the reason we hear very few words of gratitude in this world. To change this, we should remember everything that other people do for us while forgetting everything we do for others. That is the way it should be.

Even if the reward for a good deed does not come back to you directly, the person who you have done something for will feel good and this will lead to their good thoughts and deeds. Somebody who has received love will feel they should not keep it to themselves and will be prompted to do something good for another. You may never see or hear what they have done, but the love you have given will, of itself, bring about the next good deed.

The person to whom you have given love will do something good for somebody you have never seen or heard of. In this way, love takes on a life of its own and spreads from one person to another. This is a very happy thought and one I would like you all to bear in mind.

4. The Principles of Happiness

To love somebody is to practice the "love that gives," and everything I teach at IRH centers around this concept. I explain the principles of happiness as the Fourfold Path that consists of Love, Knowledge, Reflection, and Development. The path of Love, however, is pivotal.

The purpose of the path of Knowledge is to love more and more people. The more knowledge you acquire, the more useful your life becomes to more people. If you lack knowledge and intellectual power, it will be difficult for you to do good for many others. By learning extensively, you will be able to expand your range of activities, and influence even more people. This is why I say that knowledge is important—knowledge supports love.

So what about the path of Reflection? Why do we have to practice self-reflection? When you think you are practicing "the love that gives," you still need to check and see that it is the kind of love that God expects of you. There are any number of people who may think they are doing good but who have strayed from the right path. Although they may think they are practicing "the love that gives," in actual fact some of them become so blind in their acts of giving that they go as far as to spoil the recipients and eventually cause harm. The givers may have started off with pure motives but have gradually forgotten them, and come to crave recognition from others. They may now boast of the good things they have done in an effort to justify their motives. Although starting out with pure and wholesome thoughts, it is easy for the ordinary human to forget his or her original intention and stray from it. So we need to practice self-reflection in order to put ourselves back on the right course. In this way, self-reflection is practiced for the sake of love.

The fourth path of the Fourfold Path is Development, and this is also undertaken for the sake of love. When love becomes powerful, when it expresses itself strongly, it will influence more and more people. When you discover a powerful love within yourself, you will want to help as many people as possible, to create as many smiling faces and as much joy as possible. Development actually means the expansion of love. As love grows and becomes ever bigger, its ideals grow and this is what we call development.

Some may think that the Fourfold Path is hard to practice, but in the end, it all comes back to love. Knowledge, Reflection, and Development are all simply ways of making love stronger, bigger, and more wonderful.

The most basic principle that the members of IRH are required to follow is "Exploration of Right Mind." This can be explained as the guidelines that each and every member has to follow. To use a slightly old-fashioned expression, it might be called a commandment. The idea behind this can be summed up as follows: "If you wish to achieve spiritual development through the study of the Laws of Truth at the IRH, as a minimum requirement, you must have an attitude of exploring Right Mind." This means that in order to have good intentions and express them in action, you have to establish a basic stance, the attitude of exploring Right Mind.

Let me sum up: The act of giving love is what God expects of us. The work of giving love to others on God's behalf, acting as a part of Him, is more important than any other task in the world. If we have been assigned such an important job, we must reflect on ourselves daily and check to ensure that we are not thinking wrong thoughts or becoming carried away with wrong actions. This is our holy duty. If we are to become a part of God, to become His representatives and carry out the allotted task, we must remind ourselves daily of how vital it is that we do a good job, holding to the precept, "Exploring Right Mind."

The task of carrying a bouquet of love and offering every passer-by you meet a flower for free requires qualifications. If you go about this work in a mistaken state of mind, then the flowers are no longer free, nor do they fill the recipient with happiness. For this reason, you must always work to explore the quality we call Right Mind.

III. Practicing Spiritually Nurturing Love

I would like now to consider what it means to nurture others spiritually. This is very difficult to achieve. There is no ultimate goal where you can claim you have successfully brought out the best in a person. It may be possible to guide a person in a nurturing way on a one-to-one basis, if you work hard. However, when it comes to nurturing many, it requires unlimited ability. No matter how capable you may be, unfortunately, it is not easy to encourage the growth of a large number of people in a way that is appropriate to each and every individual.

There are two conditions that are required for nurturing others. The first is intelligence or knowledge, being resourceful and capable of thinking in many different ways. To consider what you can do to help a person to improve, it is necessary to have a wide range of knowledge you can draw on. Also, you need to be able to foresee the results when you act in a certain way on the basis of these resources.

If you are incapable of foreseeing how a person will react to something you do, if you cannot tell how they will react to a particular teaching, or understand what the results of your efforts may be—in other words, if you cannot understand the process of cause and effect—you will never be able to guide others rightly.

Actually, the Knowledge which I teach as part of the Four-fold Path can be referred to as the ability to see through and understand the process of cause and effect. You have to be able to see the relationship between the seeds you sow now and the harvest you will gather later. This ability can be gained through reading various books or obtaining a wide range of information.

Another important requirement in nurturing others spiritually is experience. Of course, in order to gain experience, it is often necessary to attempt to do things, going through a process of trial and error, and in many cases this will result in failure. If nothing else, at least this will teach you how not to do things. However, there are a limited number of patterns that affect the way that people think and act in particular situations. After you have built up a certain degree of experience, you will be able to recognize how people react to a particular set of circumstances. The more experience you are able to acquire, the greater the number of people you will be able to assist in their growth. Such experiences include not only success but also failure. If you have experienced a failure at some point in your life as a result of something that happened, when you see somebody facing a similar situation, you will be able to warn them of the possible danger.

To increase your knowledge and widen your experience, these are the two secrets about practicing spiritually nurturing love. In order to build the stature that enables you to do this, if you are a company executive or teacher, for example, either you have to have an intellect that has been developed through education or have a large stock of experience you can draw upon.

If you do not possess these assets of knowledge or experience yourself, you can choose another way, utilizing these resources in someone who can help you. It is still possible for you to practice spiritually nurturing love if you can find someone who has wide knowledge and experience, who will act as your personal advisor. This option requires you to be the kind of person that somebody with a rich knowledge and experience will be willing to assist. This means that you will have to be flexible, modest, and willing to learn from others. If you are capable of this, you will be able to borrow the knowledge and experience of experts and guide others in a nurturing way.

From this we can see that it is not so hard to practice fundamental love—the love at a personal, family, and ordinary social level, i.e. the love between parent and child, between a man and a woman, or the love between friends or neighbors—and that it is possible to practice this straight away. However, spiritually nurturing love requires discipline and effort. It takes time to master. The greater the effort you put into mastering this, the greater the ability you will develop, and this is something that you must continue to work on for the remainder of your life.

Members of IRH are strongly encouraged to study the Laws of Truth. This is because in order to advance from the stage of fundamental love to that of love that nurtures, it is necessary to master a large amount of knowledge. It takes a long time to gain a wide range of experiences and there is a limit to the amount we can experience in the course of our lives. However, wisdom that can take a long time to attain through experience is already explained simply and clearly in spiritual texts, so a knowledge of Truth will endow you with an understanding of things that would otherwise take several decades to master. The more wisdom you gain, the more widely you can spread love in this world.

IV. Forgiving Love

One level higher than "spiritually nurturing love" is "forgiving love," and this is extremely difficult to practice. To be able to forgive others, it is necessary for your soul to have passed through a certain number of trials. If you are gifted and able, you should be able to learn to guide and nurture people, but the ability to forgive is not something you can acquire overnight.

You will probably do your best to avoid distress, hardship, sadness, and pain; this is only natural and to be expected. However, all these factors that appear negative will turn out to be advantageous when you face a situation that requires forgiveness. Even if you are blessed with great gifts and ability, you need to have passed through adverse circumstances, hardship and privations before your true strength can shine. In the same way that iron has to be heated, forged, and then tempered before it can become a sword, people need to have passed through a variety of experiences and hardships before they can reach the state where they are able to forgive others.

I would like to say that even though you may have made many mistakes in the past, there is still a way to turn them to your advantage. The more mistaken thoughts you have had or wrong actions you have taken in the past, the greater your potential to become a good leader. To be able to forgive others, you have to have a firsthand knowledge of the hardships people pass through and understand their sorrow. It is very difficult to try and forgive others if you do not understand why they are suffering.

At the stage of mastering spiritually nurturing love, it is important to respect the idea of justice, in other words, you have to learn how to discriminate between right and wrong. Leaders need to teach others that they should cast out what is wrong and choose what is right. As you continue to make this kind of effort, you can develop yourself as a leader.

However, there is a state that goes even beyond this, because people who are in the throes of spiritual training need to be looked after. There are some people who drop out in the middle and give up their training, who are diverted or who stumble. If there was not something or someone that enfolds everyone, then people would no longer be able to believe that this world and human beings were the creation of God. If He only smiled on those who were successful and not on those who failed, if He only loved people who obeyed his commandments and not those who either broke them or failed in their attempt at obedience, then people would no longer be able to trust this world.

The majority of people are learning to cast aside evil and choose good on a limited scale, but on a much larger scale there is a great love that enfolds them all. It is this love that allows people to live as human beings, and continue their lives in this world.

The high spirits are teaching us that we should choose what is good, take what is right, and move toward God. However, in the world that exists after this, there is a place called Hell where Satan and the malicious spirits live. These evil fiends keep on coming back to Earth to lead people astray and cause them to suffer.

These spirits in Hell are the ones who failed the trials of life, like students who dropped out of school. You might think that this world would be a much better place if these spirits were destroyed, but actually they are allowed to carry on their lives and continue their negative activities. This demonstrates the great spirit of forgiveness that transcends the good and the bad we see in everyday life.

This great compassion is not unrelated to you; just consider what happens to you when you make mistakes. It is a fact of life that everybody fails to achieve their goals at times. If only those who were successful were saved and all those who failed were left to perish, then the human race would have become extinct long ago. However, we are continually given another chance, and this is something we should all be thankful for; this encourages us. The knowledge that although you may not succeed this time you will be given another chance, that you have the rest of eternity in which to improve, should provide you with the courage to do your utmost.

You should understand that the state of forgiveness is much higher than that of spiritually nurturing others; it is a step closer to the state of God. At the stage of spiritually nurturing others, you must have the knowledge to distinguish good from bad, and right from wrong. However, you also need to realize there is something more encompassing that goes beyond this distinction.

In order to reach this state, it is necessary for your spirit to be incarnated in this world hundreds, even thousands of times, and to experience difficulties and face setbacks. These experiences will enable you to sympathize when you witness the pain and sadness of countless others. Only after you have passed through numerous difficulties will you find compassion wells up within you.

It can be said that generally, love is an egalitarian force that spreads horizontally while compassion flows vertically from top to bottom. Compassion flows from the very highest realm to the lowest. As we continue to improve spiritually through self-discipline, we will gradually acquire a greater power to love. The spiritual sustenance we have gained for our souls during the course of numerous reincarnations will transform into a power that adds to the great river of love, which originates in God and runs through all dimensions.

Compassion is the heart that never stops loving others. It is like a wellspring that never runs dry. To attain this state, you will have to pass through numerous ordeals and while doing so you must be thankful for each trial as it comes, telling yourself that it is a blessing and is actually polishing your soul. In fact, in my philosophy of "Invincible Thinking," I teach that every experience you have in this world can be turned into something positive. If you see your life from a longer-term perspective, rather than the few decades you spend in this world, you will see this is true.

Even if you are studying the Laws of Truth and struggling day and night to improve yourself, you may sometimes find yourself faced with difficulties. You may ask yourself why you should be tried so sorely. But rather than complain, you need to understand that you are in fact being given a great chance to develop.

It is easy for people who are successful to guide and nurture others, but in order to forgive it is necessary to have passed through both success and failure. Once you have learned from both success and failure, you will develop great stature, filled with love, and become able to forgive every person you come into contact with. This is what God wishes of us, and we should never forget this.

Part Two

The Spirit on the Journey
to Independence

I. Starting from the Ordinary

Among the many books I have written is one entitled "Starting from the Ordinary." In this book, I present the story of my own life almost in the form of an autobiography, with the hope that it may provide a ray of hope for people who have yet to encounter the Truth, those who have not yet awoken to the true meaning of life and their mission in this world, and who regard themselves as ordinary. I hope that my experiences serve as an example for them to follow if they want to find a path toward the light through their own efforts.

The main themes of the book are the importance of spiritual discipline and aspiring for enlightenment. Rather than explaining what enlightenment is, I concentrate on describing the process for arriving at the gateway that leads to it, and I think you will find some points you can use as guides. The book was written not only for my readers, but also as a reminder to myself not to become self-satisfied. Whenever I read this book, I am reminded of the importance of returning to the basics, from where I started out.

I wrote this book in June 1988 and since then the Institute for Research in Human Happiness, of which I am the president, has grown significantly. As the Institute has grown in size and influence, I too have had to change accordingly, which has resulted in changes in the way I express my thoughts through actions and speech. However, it is always true that no matter what we do, we must never forget our beginnings and we should try to return to the basics, otherwise we will stray from the right path. I myself strongly believe this truth.

The following chapters were originally presented as a lecture on the book "Starting from the Ordinary"; I hope they will provide you with some useful clues for enriching your own life.

1. Sustaining a Thought

When I was about ten years old, I had two ambitions. One was to become a university professor—I had strong desire to have a career in the academic world. The other was to become a diplomat; this ambition was as strong as the first. I did not know why I had two such distinct dreams, but they stayed with me for the next ten years. It was not until I entered my present calling that I understood that two distinct souls existed within me and that this was the main reason for my dual aspirations. One of these souls was meditative and the other outgoing. Because these two different spirits existed within me, I developed both introverted and extroverted tendencies, and these began to manifest themselves when I was still in my teens.

Although the outcome was not quite as I had anticipated, both dreams have actually come true. If you can sustain the same vision for ten or twenty years, it will eventually have to take shape. Reading books on self-realization and personal success, I was impressed that some people were able to realize their dreams using will power, and having experienced this for myself, I am convinced that it is true.

Anyone can have ambitions or dreams for a short while, but very few people are able to sustain them for a prolonged period. Strange as it may seem, I think the reason for this is that people tend to regard themselves as in some way exceptional. One characteristic common to those who consider themselves gifted or clever is that they are easily distracted. They keep turning their attention to something new, and have a tendency to try their hand at numerous things. As a result, very few of them achieve a real success. Their attention keeps flitting from subject to subject, not allowing them to concentrate on one single theme.

The same is true of children. Unusually clever children are fascinated by changes in their environment and are easily stimulated by change. As a result, however, they find it difficult to stick to one thing. They are inclined to keep changing, moving from one game to the next. On the other hand, children who somehow know they are not so clever will focus so much on a single game they tend to ignore what happens around them. These children may appear dull or mediocre to their parents or friends; but, contrary to expectations, in the long term this tenacity and holding on to one thought can give rise to amazing transformations.

2. Improvement Through Effort

i) An environment suitable for introspection

When I was a child, my family lived in a small house, but there was an annex to it. After dinner I would pick up my school bag and head for this other building to study. It did not stand on the same plot of land so I had to walk about two hundred yards down the road and around a corner to get there.

The ground floor had once been used as a factory, but by that time it was unused. I would pass straight through this and up the stairs to a room on the second floor. When I turned the light on, I would see big spiders and other insects scuttling for cover and I always thought it a rather scary place. The building backed onto an uncultivated valley and lots of creatures used to find their way in. There were grasshoppers and even snakes, so I always had to be careful when I entered.

I started to use this room for my studies from the age of about ten or eleven, and one result of this was that I began to develop a habit of contemplating different subjects on my own. Having read a large number of biographies and autobiographies, I realize now that the majority of great writers and thinkers had a private place they used to go to as children. One of the most famous Japanese authors, Soseki Natsume (1867–1916) wrote, "as a child I often used to go into the storehouse and play by myself." It was a place where the family's valuables were kept and he would go in to read books, look at picture scrolls, or study the family's collection of ceramics. The result of this was that he grew up to have a rather unique way about him.

There is no telling what is going to stand us in good stead later in our lives. I thought that I started to practice meditation when I was about twenty years old, but I later realized that I had started to prepare myself for it while I was still in primary school. Even now, I can remember writing poetry while listening to the sounds of the insects in that room where numerous creatures came to visit me.

The room had no heating and so in the winter I would wear a jacket, wrap my legs up in an old blanket, and wear gloves, a hat, and a mask in an effort to keep warm. I imagine that there is hardly anybody today who has to hold their pencil in a gloved hand or wear a mask to try and keep the cold at bay even in the middle of winter, but my room was so drafty that I had no choice but to dress like this to do my studies.

Although I was studying regular school subjects such as geography or world history, I was able to experience something of what a monk must feel. I had an indescribable respect for the experience that came from spiritual discipline. Perhaps some of my readers have experienced a similar feeling—due to hidden memories of past lives as monks or nuns. People who have undergone religious training in a past life will retain an unconscious respect for spiritual discipline.

The belief that it is indescribably valuable to exert yourself for a noble cause is not something that can be learned; these kinds of values are something you have to be born with. It is a feeling that people awaken to as children, which grows steadily until it becomes firmly established as part of their character. If you look back over your life and realize that you have experienced this kind of feeling at some time, this is proof that in past lives you underwent spiritual training.

I would say that people who enjoy spiritual training for its own sake, without understanding its goal, were born in the ages without the Great Guiding Spirits of Light, when there were only disciples in charge. During these periods, aspirants were constantly taught that spiritual training was an end unto itself, and would undergo it without really understanding the reason.

People who understand clearly why they should undergo training are those who lived at a time when one of the Great Guiding Spirits was teaching on Earth. On the other hand, those who do not have a proper understanding but enjoy spiritual discipline anyway were born when the disciples of the Great Spirits were in charge and studied under them. If you reflect deeply, you will be able to recognize which group you belong to.

ii) Self-mastery is the greatest ability of all
I learned self-mastery at an early age, and I believe it was very important for my development. As I reflect on my childhood, I see that the reason I learned this was that I felt my own incompleteness keenly and was not satisfied with who I was. I had a very strong motivation to do something to improve myself.

Self-mastery is an ability in itself. There are other kinds of abilities that are more obvious, but the desire to improve oneself and overcome weaknesses, self-mastery in other words, is a very valuable quality. In a sense, it could even be said that this ability is all-powerful. It is not something you are taught in school or in the workplace, but this ability means that you become the master of yourself. If you are capable of this, it will help you open up many new possibilities.

Sometimes you may be surprised by a totally unexpected sight in nature. For example, water may be welling up from an obviously improbable place such as a crack in a rock, or grass flourishing on top of a boulder. As nature teaches us in these instances, with the ability to master yourself, you will be able to overcome any difficulties you face and find a way out.

If you have children, you may be wondering what kind of educational opportunities you can offer them. Perhaps you provide music or sport lessons, according to their strengths. However, if all you think about is technique and results of these lessons, it will not be sufficient. It is more important to teach them about the essential spirit that lies behind any training, that is to say, the importance of the spiritual attitude of overcoming one's own weaknesses and becoming a magnificent human being. This is the greatest gift that parents can give their children, and it will stand them in good stead even if they have to leave this world before they are fully grown.

When I was a child I used to tell myself that even if I could not achieve as much in one hour as somebody else, if I stuck at it for three or four hours, I would be able to catch up with them. I also thought that if somebody got tired of something after one year, but I did not give up and carried on working on the same thing for four or five years, I would be able to catch up with them. I believe this sort of thinking forms the basis of my philosophy.

Before I got to where I am now, I took a lot of detours. Although I sometimes thought of these simply as wasted effort, I now realize that in fact they served to increase the capacity of my soul. At a certain point in time, continued effort gives rise to a remarkable change in a person's situation; often, it is as if a chemical reaction has occurred. There is no telling when this will happen, but if you continue to apply yourself to something meaningful, eventually this will open a new path for you to move forward on.

3. The Extraordinary Within the Ordinary
i) Radiating light

When I was young, I used to think that if I continued to shine, no matter how small my personal world, no matter how modest my environment, then that would bring great hope and opportunities. I still believe this is true. Many people may feel they have not been blessed with an ideal environment or circumstances. But they should not dream of rising to instant stardom. No matter how small the world they inhabit, they should work to strengthen their light in their current environment or in the position they occupy now.

Let me take an example to explain this further. A diamond will attract the eyes of people to it, even if it is dropped on a riverbank. If its light is obscured in some way, or its surface becomes dirty, it may be left alone and become buried. But if it shines brightly enough, it will eventually be found and put in a more suitable place. There is always a response to light.

In my book, *The Starting Point of Happiness*[2] I wrote about "meeting someone who is precious to you." A lot of people in this world are actually on the lookout for people of ability to help them, and although you may not realize it, somewhere, somebody may even now be evaluating your stature. Somebody who is not necessarily connected with the career in which you are trying to progress may see you in a completely different light and help open a new path for you. This is the wonder of meeting a "precious" person. As there is always this possibility, it is essential that you radiate a powerful aura of light. If a meeting like this does not happen for you, then you should infer that it is because your light is too small and weak.

ii) From self-mastery to love

A person who has been discovered by somebody else and given the opportunity to succeed will want to discover someone else who is talented, to bring them out of the stagnation of a banal life and help lift them to the heights of the exceptional. This is a characteristic of people who have learned to shine through their own efforts.

There are others in this world who seem to believe they are special, and have been born superior to others. One characteristic of this kind of illusion is that they tend to be cold toward others, even to the extent of ignoring their very existence. They behave is as if they were walking down a street, totally ignoring the ants and other tiny forms of life that exist under their feet.

On the other hand, people who have managed to climb out of a stagnant and banal life as a result of their own efforts cannot

---

2. *The Starting Point of Happiness*, Lantern Books (2000).

remain indifferent to others. They share a strong desire to find others who are trapped in the silt of mediocrity, just as they themselves once were, to help them. This is how the spirit of self-development and diligence is transformed into love. Although you may be successful in self-mastery and make a constant effort to achieve your goals, if the fruits of your diligence do not bring others happiness, it has been in vain. People who only think of themselves and use a strong will solely for personal progress will find themselves leading very lonely lives when they become old.

Those who have achieved a good position in society but whose later years are very lonely, who have been cast aside by friends and family alike, perhaps devoted their entire lives to searching for personal gain and neglected to give love to others. They probably did not make much effort to help others achieve their full potential, although they may have had ample opportunity to do so. Those who complain that despite their brilliant personal record they have suffered greatly through adversity will no doubt find that this applies to them. People who have become very powerful but who, in radiating their light, have overshadowed numerous others and caused them to suffer will find that this kind of end awaits them. Those who consider themselves naturally outstanding will think they deserve special treatment, that they should be in the limelight. If they carry on this way, they will eventually meet a very cold and sad end.

On the other hand, those who think of themselves as quite ordinary but lucky enough to be able to shine through their own efforts will always remain humble. They will feel that the main reason they were able to get ahead in the world was because they received the help of countless others and, as a result, will never forget the gratitude they feel. To go out into the world and be successful, you must make sure that you never lose your humility and gratitude.

There are a lot of people with talent, but not all of them will necessarily be successful. The reason for this is that many will become so infatuated with their own abilities they will lose their humility. As soon as this happens, they become prone to setbacks. When they forget their gratitude to others, they become immersed in their own world, which leads to isolation. Basically, the problem is that, if they are in danger, there will be nobody around to stretch out a hand and help them.

iii) Preventing a fall

There are ambitious people who succeed in rising to the heights of glory through their own strenuous efforts. However, if they allow themselves to become self-satisfied and proud of their own ability, forgetting gratitude and humility, the place they will go after death will be the realm of the self-centered. This is the place for those who do not think of others and are only ever concerned with their own reputation. It is for people who show no more concern for others than they do for the scenery seen from the window of a passing train.

You may have heard the story of the "North Wind and the Sun." The North Wind tries to remove a traveler's coat by force, but fails. The sun, however, is able to achieve victory simply by smiling gently on the man. Similar situations can occur in real life. Rather than think only of yourself and end up in the realm of the self-centered after death, surely it is much better to start out ordinary and concentrate on becoming a person who is full of love. When you set out to achieve this goal, it is important to focus on "building results."

For the first three years after I established IRH, I adopted an extremely cautious attitude and applied to myself and every member a policy of steadily building up results. I refrained from expanding the membership too quickly, without a solid basis. I continued to say, "It is impossible to achieve sudden success. Even if you happen to achieve something remarkable in a short space of time, this kind of success is usually short-lived. It is much more prudent to concentrate on building strength little by little."

Even if you are talented and have a great potential, if you are a large diamond, you will not be able to give out a brilliant light until you have undergone a long and steady process of polishing. Moreover, even after you start to sparkle, the light will soon dim unless you are polished regularly.

Human beings are all children of God, and we all have a divine nature within. However, until you awaken to this truth and restore this original purity, until you begin to give out your own divine light through your efforts to polish yourself, you remain simply an ordinary person, who started this earthly life as a baby with nothing. You should never forget this truth. Let me repeat that no matter who you are, even if you are a Great Guiding Spirit of Light, you have to start out in this world with nothing. This is one of the fundamentals of the Laws of Truth.

Even if you achieve success once or twice and become the focus of attention, if you allow yourself to be filled with pride, your fame will be short-lived. People who do this are over-optimistic. Actually, if you read the Buddhist scriptures, you will find that Shakyamuni Buddha repeatedly warned people to beware of a fall as a result of inflated pride.

We human beings can easily fall into the trap of thinking that we know it all, and that we are someone special. So, unless we remind ourselves that every single person, no matter who it may be, has to start from nothing, and that to achieve success in this world we need to walk along steadily the path, we will fall into the trap of thinking we are exceptional simply because we have managed to achieve some minor success. The result of this deluded thinking is that, instead of giving love, we take love from others, and this is something that we must always remain on our guard against.

4. Discovery
i) Discovery gives you the chance to leap ahead
There is a precious secret to be treasured that allows ordinary people become outstanding, promising members of society who can contribute to the world. This treasure is called "discovery."

It is essential that you discover something new every day, every year. People who simply drift through life without any particular purpose will only create a future that befits their attitude. But those who never cease to make discoveries will have a future filled with growth and development.

It was quite a long time ago now that a management seminar was organized by Matsushita Electric Industry (known outside Japan as Panasonic) for leaders of Japanese industry. The speaker was Konosuke Matsushita (1894–1989), the founder of this company, and the audience came to hear the secret of his great success. Konosuke made a presentation about his "dam management" theory, suggesting that a business corporation never knows when it will meet a crisis and it is therefore essential to keep ample reserves on hand, like water that is kept back in a dam. He said that unless ample resources were stored like a reservoir full of water it would be impossible to cope with emergencies.

Following his talk, when the time came for questions and answers, somebody asked for a practical explanation of how this "dam management" philosophy should be undertaken. But Konosuke only said bluntly, "That is a question to which I do not know the answer. The only thing I can say is that unless you want to do this, you will be unable to achieve it." This reply resulted in a lot of disappointment; the audience found it very difficult to believe that somebody as great as Konosuke Matsushita would give such a vague reply. Naturally, they were expecting a clear explanation of how this philosophy could be put into practice.

The meeting broke down as everybody started to talk, but among the delegates there was one person who understood exactly what Matsushita had meant. This man was Kazuo Inamori, the founder of the Kyocera Corporation. He decided to put what he had learned that day into practice, and this decision later resulted in the remarkable success of his company. Inamori understood that success depends upon the kinds of thoughts one entertains. The majority of the audience thought that the seminar had been a waste of time, and that if Matsushita did not know how to practice what he preached, he should not have called them all together in the first place. Indeed, Inamori was the only person who really understood the secret of Matsushita's success.

As you can see, by discovering something that everyone else overlooks, and absorbing a new idea that enhances your own philosophy, it is possible to make a great leap forward. I do not know how many people were able to pick up clues from this particular lecture by Konosuke Matsushita and the subsequent question and answer session but, at the very least, it resulted in the record success of one particular company, Kyocera Corporation.

This episode clearly indicates that actually everything begins with what you think. It is possible for a seed of thought to produce great success, or it can grow into a factor that obstructs development. Everything begins with a thought—this is not just an expression. I know from experience that it is true.

ii) Accumulate discoveries and wisdom

The same can happen to those who listen to my lectures. You may find that a particular phrase strikes a chord in your heart. I have no way of knowing if what I have said will have this effect, but if you experience it, like digging for gold and striking a nugget, then it is a moment to be treasured.

These moments of discovery are different from person to person, and what will act as an important keyword for you may mean nothing to someone else. The same can be said of reading books; but it is a fact that sometimes a single discovery can have a great effect on a person's life.

Looking at those who become leaders and guide others, it is obvious that their knowledge is not limited to what they learned at school; rather, they have a wisdom that comes from discoveries they have made through numerous experiences. It is this wisdom that gives their characters the depth and strength to enable them to lead others.

You may have had the chance to listen to talks given by lecturers belonging to the Institute for Research in Human Happiness. Whatever you may gain from their talks comes from the valuable discoveries they have made in the course of their lives. A talk given by somebody who has accumulated wisdom through discoveries, taking advantage of every possible opportunity in everyday life, is often very insightful. On the other hand, the speech of someone who has not discovered much will sound somewhat bland and shallow. Whether the speakers have lived aimlessly or have made many meaningful discoveries will gradually be reflected in the popularity of the lecturers.

Experience does not mean simply growing older, it is the sum total of everything a person is able to discover and grasp in the course of a life. I would like to point out to young people especially that, with regard to discoveries, careful observation is most important. When you are still young your mind is sharp and so it is easier to absorb knowledge. But if you want to improve the quality of the discoveries you make, you can only do so through keen observation.

Therefore, you must observe as many people as possible carefully, for they are the source of ample information. You should study the way they think and act. You must ask yourself how a successful person would act in a particular situation, and also watch how those who fail behave when faced with the same problem. As you continue with this practice of observing others, you will be able to build up a store of knowledge without necessarily having to undergo the same experiences yourself. By watching others you can learn things that lie outside your own personal experience. This is very important to remember.

iii) Learn through empathy
People's opinions differ from person to person, but when you hear something that you think rings true, you should adopt this view as your own. There is no such thing as a copyright on a person's views of life, so you should adopt everything you think is good and incorporate it into your own views. Although an idea may have originally been somebody else's, if you sympathize with what the person said, it means that something similar already existed within you without your realizing it. If this potential had not existed within you to begin with, it would not have sounded true.

So, if you gather together the parts of the opinions of others that you sympathize with, you can incorporate them to enhance your own philosophy. When the person who gives and the person who receives have a sympathetic response to one another, it means that to a certain degree they share the same qualities.

To learn from somebody else's outlook on life is certainly not the same as copying or mimicking that person. If you feel a strong sympathetic response to something someone says, it means that something of the same already exists within you. So, you should take every opportunity to study as many people as possible, then express what you have learned in your own words. If you do not do this, but simply sit and think without trying to learn from every opportunity that presents itself, you will not be able to achieve anything meaningful. You must learn from the knowledge, experiences, and words of others, then assimilate them to enrich yourself.

If you are a member of IRH and you read spiritual truths over and over, you will often find yourself quoting what you have read. This is fine, and it shows that the parts you often quote are in the process of becoming parts of your own personal philosophy. In this way, people are able to grow infinitely. If you pay no attention to the opinions of others and think that it is sufficient simply to express your own thoughts, you will never be able to enrich yourself with a wealth of wisdom; in fact, your views will become increasingly limited. Like a plant, if your mind uses up all the available nutrition, it will not flourish and never come to bloom. Like a cut flower in a vase, it may bloom briefly but it will eventually die. If a flower is to thrive, it has to put roots down into the earth to absorb nourishment and water. In the same way, you must learn from others to obtain the nourishment and water that your soul requires.

It is important that you take every opportunity to learn from others as it is only in this way that you will be able to discover the very best that exists within yourself. If you hope to find treasure that has been hidden in the ground, you need tools. Knowledge and experience are like shovels or spades and it is through study that these tools are created. It is through learning from others that you are able to create the tools which will allow you to discover the treasures hidden within you.

5. Determination and Courage

Courage is not something you can learn at school or through work, and it is very important. We generally climb the stairs of life one step at a time; but if we summon up courage, it is possible to make huge leaps. With courage, even those who you would never have imagined could amount to much are capable of making giant leaps.

Those who are talented but who find it difficult to get ahead are probably lacking courage. Courage springs from strong determination, and determination is born of making a choice when it is necessary to do so. Although there may be numerous paths that lead to success, you have only a single body and therefore you can only proceed down a single road. If you are faced with a variety of ways forward, you must choose which one to take, and you only have one choice. You have to be brave when you must make a decision.

To make a choice means to abandon all the other possibilities. In order to find the courage to make your choice, you have to know which way to abandon and which to follow. To make a vital choice that will determine your course of life, you have to cast other possibilities away. It is impossible to take everything, so you have to decide which possibilities to ignore and which to take.

II. Independence

1. Responsibility and Personal Stature

A spirit of independence is extremely important if you wish to continue to grow. Independence is, in other words, the desire to develop your character and uniqueness to the furthest limits. However, independence can give rise to some difficult problems, and one of these is how to stay in harmony with others while you strive to exert your personality to the full.

I would like you to be aware that while it is fine to be independent, if it results in your disturbing the harmony of the people around you, it may indicate irresponsibility. When those who are irresponsible have an independent lifestyle, it can often bring suffering to those around, so it is essential to have a keen sense of responsibility.

There are a variety of criteria by which a person's stature may be measured and one of these is the willingness to take responsibility for what you do. In other words, if you want to know what kind of person you are, what position you occupy in society, and what your stature is, then you simply have to consider to what extent you are prepared to accept responsibility. This is an extremely important point because people are usually less willing to do this than they like to think.

By taking responsibility, I mean not only being responsible for your own life, but also for the lives of others, and this is the vital quality required of a leader. The number of people you are willing to take responsibility for shows whether or not you possess the stature of a leader. People who have an irresponsible leader will have difficult lives indeed.

When it comes to taking responsibility, you must first look at your own situation in a totally honest way. If you feel you have failed at what you have been doing, then you must admit that this is your responsibility. Only then will you find the next step to take. However, if instead you try to place the blame on the people around you or on external conditions, then you will never be able to improve your lot. The ability to admit to a mistake, even if it puts you in an awkward position, is indispensable in allowing you to develop a powerful spirit of independence.

When you have made a mistake, it is only natural not to want to take responsibility for it and instead to try and blame all sorts of external factors. Actually, there may be some truth in this, and if causes are analyzed, you find it is not usually the fault of any one person; everybody involved has a share of the blame. That is why people like to comfort themselves by saying that a mistake is the result of various external factors, which they use in their defense. This is quite a natural reaction and unless you think in this way, a failure may make you very nervous and cause you to worry endlessly.

However, you will never be impressed by people who try to justify their failures. On the other hand, someone who can take responsibility beyond what is expected can appear quite exceptional. It is easy to apply this to someone else, but very difficult for us to apply it to ourselves; however, I would like you all to try and make the effort.

BUSINESS REPLY MAIL

FIRST-CLASS MAIL PERMIT NO. 7325   NEW YORK, NY

POSTAGE WILL BE PAID BY ADDRESSEE

Lantern Books
1 Union Square West, Suite 201
New York, NY 10003

✓ Yes! I want to become happy!

Please send me a free booklet by Ryuho Okawa with clues that will help me attain true happiness—NOW!

Name: Mr / Mrs / Ms / Miss _____

Address: _____

City: _____ State: _____ ZIP: _____

SEND THIS CARD OR FAX TO IRH NEW YORK AT (201) 461-7278 OR YOUR NEAREST IRH BRANCH LISTED AT THE BACK OF THIS BOOK NOW!!

THANK YOU FOR YOUR INTEREST IN LANTERN BOOKS.

It is usually clear whether or not you have done something which has directly caused a problem, and sometimes you may be able to avoid taking direct responsibility for an accident. You may be able to say quite honestly that it was not your fault, but there is such a thing as "indirect responsibility."

Let me take the example of a mother whose son falls when he is playing in a park with friends. All she can think of may be to blame a neighbor's child, but there is another way of looking at this situation. She could also think that although it was because his friend pushed him that her son fell and hurt himself, she is also to be blamed because she was not aware of a potential danger that existed. In this way, she can take greater responsibility. If the mother thinks to herself, "It is my fault that my son fell. I was so busy chatting with the mothers that I was not paying attention to him, and that's when the accident occurred," then she can avoid blaming others. If you admit that you share the responsibility for what happened, then you will not want to place the blame on others.

Taking responsibility is very strongly connected to the practice of self-reflection based on the Eightfold Path, particularly "Right Speech," where you are required to examine whether you have hurt others with your words. If you think that somebody else is to blame, you are likely to say something that could hurt that person. However, if at the very moment you are about to speak, you can pause and think that you have at least a secondary responsibility for what has happened, you can avoid speaking sharply. Even if you do speak your mind, it will take a softer form. It is not easy to put this into actual practice; but being aware of this truth is a good starting point, otherwise you will never learn to take responsibility. Then, the next step is that you make an effort to enlarge the extent of the responsibility you feel prepared to take. As you continue in this discipline, what you thought of initially as responsibility will eventually be transformed into love. This is guaranteed to happen.

2. Overcoming Failures

You can learn a lot from failure. Even if the failure is not your own, everything that happens around you will always provide you with some lesson. So it is essential that you learn from other people's failures. If you have this kind of attitude, you are practicing what I call "Invincible Thinking," and through it you will be able to win in every situation in this life. Faced with a failure caused by someone else, if you simply conclude that it has nothing to do with you and that it is not your problem, you will learn nothing. On the other hand, if you admit that it has some relevance to you, you can always learn something through an analysis of the incident. After all, a person of great character is someone who has learned as many lessons as possible from the book of life.

When you have experienced a failure or witnessed someone else's, you must analyze the situation carefully to understand why and how it happened, so it will never happen again. Take precautions to ensure that you never fall into the same pattern of failure again. It is essential to master this way of thinking because it enables you to find the basic causes of unhappiness and the key to change unhappiness into happiness. Viewed from the perspective of a disinterested third party, mistakes and unhappiness generally have their source in the repetition of the same old mistakes. When looked at from the outside this is easy to understand; but when you are personally involved, you are often unable to see yourself objectively.

When you recognize that you are about to fall into the same old pattern that leads to failure, you must learn to stop right there. Please reflect on yourself and remember what happens when you start talking in a certain way, examining your own tendencies and analyzing the pattern. Then, if you find yourself saying something similar again in the future, you will be able to recognize the impending danger and prevent it. However, many people repeat the same mistakes over and over again, becoming no wiser as a result of their past experiences. If they have suffered some particularly crushing failure in the past, the moment they register the first signs of the pattern repeating itself they act as if they have already repeated the mistake. It is like a person who, upon seeing somebody sneeze, assumes that it is influenza, then, before they know it, starts to shiver and behave as if they had caught the disease. Failure can actually become a conditioned reflex.

To achieve happiness, it is necessary to overcome this negative tendency by any means available. You must look back over the pattern of your past mistakes and analyze how you tend to react in particular situations and what the results are. In this way you will be able to recognize when you are about to fall into a familiar pattern and take the necessary steps to ensure you do not repeat the same mistake again. When you see a potential mistake, pause and try to react the opposite way to the way you did before. You must tell yourself that you are not going to let it happen, that you are not going to end up in the same situation again.

Everybody has their own patterns of failure, and only the will power of each individual can break such patterns. For example, if you believe in your subconscious that you are about to make another mistake or suffer some setback, if you are scared that you may annoy a person who holds a key position in your plans, then these thoughts are sufficient to make things turn out exactly as you feared. However, if you are successful in canceling out such negative thoughts using your will power, the situation will improve.

The same can be said of personal interactions. Once you have experienced a setback in a relationship with one person, you tend to believe that everybody behaves in the same way, so as soon as you see the first signs of an impending rupture, you assume you are going to spoil a relationship again or that it will end in harsh words. When this happens, you must tell yourself that your fear is ungrounded and that different people react to situations in different ways. Even somebody who was angry with you yesterday will not necessarily be angry with you today; in fact they may even compliment you. If you think that just because they were angry with you yesterday they will be angry again today and you react by behaving sheepishly, this will only annoy them and lead to a repetition of the previous day's row. You must convince yourself that each day is different; it is as if we are given a new life every day.

3. Truth and Economics
i) The relationship between financial conditions and mental tendencies
I would like to consider now your feelings about money; because financial matters are closely connected to a person's independence. Unfortunately, those who are involved in the search for spiritual blessings are often lacking in financial acumen. Those who have a subconscious affinity with poverty will actually experience poverty, because what is in the realm of the mind will inevitably materialize in this world on Earth. For this reason, it is very important to examine your own mental tendencies carefully. People who subconsciously believe that money is evil will find that their wealth slips between their fingers. As a result, even though they may have an income, they will be incapable of holding onto it and will squander it all.

For each person, there is a specific upper limit to the amount of money they feel comfortable with. Some are timid and feel uncomfortable if they carry more than a few hundred dollars. They worry it will be stolen by a pickpocket, that they might drop it or use it to gamble. There are others who never keep more than twenty dollars in their wallet, and those who become nervous when they have more than a certain amount of money in the bank, worrying they might be tempted to get involved in speculating. They feel guilt or unease if they possess more than this amount and, as a result, they are never able to save much money. Moreover, there are even people who are not happy unless they are actually in debt. A certain percentage of people are only happy when they have borrowed money and tell themselves that they will not be able to die until they have paid off what they owe, with their debts acting as an incentive to work.

Thoughts, however, always come before the actions and so the first thing you should do to avoid falling into this kind of trap is to check on the way you are thinking. You will see that your thoughts work in patterns especially when it comes to finance. People who feel guilty about being rich will always end up poor. As soon as they start to make much profit, they begin to suspect that it is some kind of a mistake, and convince themselves they will never die peacefully. Before they know it, they have lost all they had made as a result of an accident of some sort. Although they may be wealthy in the short-term, their prosperity will not last.

To avoid being like them, you must make your own plans for the future to contribute to the creation of a better world, according to the wealth you manage to acquire. You need to draw a picture on the canvas in your mind, and make clear plans for yourself about what you will do when you have achieved wealth. If you limit your plans to the domestic scale, they will remain small; but if you want to form a plan to use any extra income, draw a clear picture of the future, and become perfectly convinced of its appropriateness, then it will no longer appear wrong for you to accumulate wealth.

This is no laughing matter, as there are people who continually suffer unhappiness as a result of economic difficulties. A shortage of money can create so much stress that it can result in digestive problems. Thoughts about being unable to make a payment or to settle an overdue bill can result in insomnia that no amount of drugs will be able to cure; but as soon as the payment is made the insomnia goes away. The only way for such people to overcome this kind of complaint is to make a fundamental change in their way of thinking.

ii) Useful work and income

According to the Laws of Truth, those who have done work that is useful to others will be rewarded accordingly. Money has an exchange value, so people who are useful will be rewarded with it according to their worth. If you do not earn very much money, it means that either you are not doing something useful or you are doing what you feel like doing according to your personal desires. So you should pause and consider what would be of real use to others. Rather than thinking of ways to earn more money, first you must think about how you can contribute to the good of society at large.

If you are engaged in a job that provides a useful service, then you will naturally attract money. If you do not manage to earn enough, it may well mean that you are not of enough use to others. If the service you provide is of little use to people or is inadequate, then you will not attract much money. As a result, you will find your finances running into the red. If you are in debt, you must ask yourself if you are really providing something that is of use to people. If you are always thinking about how to provide a useful service, you will find that your earnings will eventually begin to increase.

Some people like to complain that, despite the fact they are selling good products at a reasonable price, they are unable to make any profit, or that it is because they provide too good a service that they are always poor. It is wrong to think in this way. If the public really wants something, a demand will be created. If there is no demand for an item then, even if it is well-produced, the person who makes it may be simply acting like a craftsman working only for his or her own satisfaction. It is quite irresponsible to run a business this way, so I want you all to try and ensure that this is not the mistake you are making.

To be economically blessed is definitely not a bad thing. You should not slight money. Rather, you should always remember the importance of achieving a reasonable standard of living so you can secure peace of mind for yourself.

4. Gaining Trust
In order to develop limitlessly while maintaining harmonious relationships with others, it is important to keep promises. Of course, it is not always possible to carry out a promise to the letter, but you should always be willing to keep your word with complete sincerity. If you cannot keep a promise, it is important that you feel regret and are willing to make amends at a later date.

This attitude reminds me of the word "zanshin," which is used in the Japanese martial art kendo, and which means "to leave your heart behind." Kendo is similar to fencing, only players use swords made of bamboo. I used to practice this martial art as a boy. During a kendo match, players tend to become very focused on their own moves. When you are about to deliver a blow to the opponent's head, you cannot think of anything else. If it is successful, fine, but if not, your stance is spoiled and you are left open to a blow from the opponent. I actually experienced this and learned that even when I was concentrating on my own moves with all my might, it was necessary to "leave my heart behind," or allow myself a space to think about the next move.

This attitude can be applied in human relationships. Even if we have promised to do something, it sometimes turns out to be impossible. However, you can generally tell from a person's character whether they just made an easy promise which they had no intention of keeping, or whether they did everything they could to carry out the promise, were unable to fulfill it, and would be willing to make up for it later. It is important you keep this willingness in your heart. Even if you are unable to keep your promise, you need to retain the wish to preserve the feeling of trust that exists between you and the people around you.

There are any number of situations where you will not be able to keep your word despite making every effort to do so. But you should not allow this to destroy a relationship; instead, you should determine to make up for your failure at the earliest possible opportunity. This creates the foundation for a solid relationship based on mutual trust.

III. Diverse Values

1. The Importance of Understanding

It is extremely difficult to understand human beings and one reason for devoting yourself to the study of the Laws of Truth is to gain a deep insight into people. An inability to understand others is one of the main sources of misery. Even though you may meet people who do not agree with you, if you can understand their way of thinking and the way they live, there is still the possibility of creating good relationships. On the other hand, if you are unable to understand other people at all, it will be emotionally difficult for you to accept them.

How much you know about people, that is to say your knowledge of humanity, is very important. People have all sorts of opinions. Perhaps you have all met some who come up with the strangest ideas. Of course, from their point of view, your opinions will seem equally incredible, as your outlooks are probably quite opposite. You might be happier if you were never to meet any of these people, but you cannot simply avoid it. It is important that you learn that there are many people in the world whose opinions do not concur with yours. Once you have become aware of this, you are then left with the question of how you can overcome such differences.

2. Learning from Personal Relationships

i) Learning from those who you do not like

If you meet someone who has different opinions or beliefs from yours, it is important that you do not allow this difference of opinion to prejudice you against them. A lot of people when they meet somebody with different values from themselves or somebody with whom they cannot agree on some critical point will simply conclude that they have nothing in common and make no effort to become friends. However, if they continue to think in this way, they cannot expect to reap an abundant harvest from their lives on Earth.

Human beings have a tendency to see things in black and white. We tend to believe that people with whom we feel an affinity should all think the same way as we do. So, when we see someone we get on well with being friendly toward somebody we do not like, we may feel betrayed and put an end to the friendship. This is very childish, but it is a fact that a lot of people make decisions based solely on whether they like or dislike a particular individual.

I personally do not act this way. If you allow yourself to think in terms of "yes or no," "friend or enemy," "black or white," you will find your outlook becoming very limited. You will not learn much if you have this kind of attitude. If you have an antipathy to someone, you may feel like avoiding them, and you will not want to listen to what they have to say or learn anything from them. However, it is often the case that those you do not like, or who are quite opposite to you, have the most to teach you. Perhaps you can see it is true that you had a lot more to learn from someone you disliked or who appeared to you to be a real enemy than you did from your friends.

The people you consider to be your friends are likely to think in a similar fashion to you, and so they offer less for you to learn from. On the other hand, those who you feel are not reliable and do not feel comfortable with have a lot more to teach you. You may even share certain characteristics with these people and this will give you cause for reflection. They can be teachers for you and provide you with material for study, so you must be careful not to miss the opportunities to learn lessons through relationships with them.

However, when you have this kind of attitude, you may sometimes be misunderstood, so you have to be prepared for this. Let me explain this with an example. Suppose I compliment a person; they may assume that I like them much more than others. Consequently, when they see me acting in a friendly way toward others, they may feel they are being downgraded in my estimation, and this will make them act crossly toward me. However, unless this kind of narrow view is corrected, you cannot advance from the level at which you consider love to be on a one-to-one basis to a higher level of love that radiates out in all directions.

Love develops from a one-to-one level to one-to-many, then goes beyond this until it reaches the point where it is directed toward countless people, in other words, the level known as "existence as love." The directions in which love flows must continue to increase. This is the way love develops.

Love usually begins between a limited number of people—for instance, between lovers, husband and wife, parents and children, or friends. This love is precious, but if you wish to advance in your spiritual discipline, you must not allow yourself to be limited to these relationships. It is when your love develops from a limited form to one that spreads out to embrace a wide range of people that the capacity of your soul is increased.

This means that if you aim to develop yourself infinitely, you need to try and surmount the tendency to limit your relationships to certain types of people, and you must not allow yourself to be selective about who you wish to be with. If you try to build relationships with as many different types of people as possible, you may sometimes cause confusion to those who have rather limited views. However, this kind of attitude will surely add a new richness to your life. I am sure you will meet many people who do not appreciate you, or whom you have difficulty admiring. However, you should not refuse to have anything to do with them, but try to analyze exactly what it is about them you dislike.

You may feel that it is beyond your capability to accept certain aspects of a person's character; but if you look harder, there are sure to be other aspects that are worthy of admiration. If you focus on the positive traits and make an effort to like these, your positive feelings will be transmitted to the other person. They will then become aware that you do not dislike them completely, and that although you may not be keen on certain aspects of their character, there are other parts which you do like. When they understand this, they will begin to make an effort to change. They will try to hide the part of their character you dislike when they are talking to you; their characters will gradually alter until only the good parts show. In this way, if you let the other person know that there are parts of their character you like, you can encourage them to change their personality for the better. However, if you do not give them a chance and just express your dislike for them, there can be no positive change. For this reason, it is essential you do not cut off from them completely.

ii) Keeping a psychological distance

Another problem when we meet people is deciding how much distance we want to keep. Perhaps you have come across those who try to force their way into your heart; if you open the doors to your heart, they enter. If you take one step back, they take one step forward. If you step back once more, they come forward again. If you have this type of person as a friend, you find it most distressing. The relationship starts off as friendship, but gradually they try to take over your life. They are so pushy that you want to keep them at arm's length.

It is important, therefore, that you treat friends with caution. A friendship should not be an all-or-nothing proposition. You do not need to accept everything your friends do, nor should you completely reject people who are not friends. You must always consider the distance you keep between yourself and others. There is a point beyond which you do not have to let people come, however friendly you may want to be. If you are able to keep the appropriate distance, it will make for a long-lived relationship; but if you let others get too close, you will forever be meddling in each other's lives and the friendship will soon break down.

If you make a mistake in judging the distance, you may find that the other person is getting closer and closer until you cannot stand it any longer and want to put an end to the relationship. If this happens, the other person will be at a loss to understand what went wrong. You had been so friendly to them up to that point that they cannot see why you had to turn your back on them so suddenly. This kind of person is incapable of understanding that they imposed too much on the relationship; so it is important, from the beginning, to allow an appropriate distance.

Those who are devoted to spiritual discipline should always keep a little more distance from those who are not. As you

advance in spiritual training, you will become less and less likely
to share the opinions of those who are not interested in spirituality. A difference in spiritual awareness results in different ways
of looking at the world, but this is something you must simply
accept. The secret of maintaining harmonious relationships with
many is to keep an appropriate psychological distance.

However, if you find the other person has a similar level of
spiritual awareness to you, you will be able to understand one
another on a very deep level—a level of friendship that you are
very unlikely to reach through ordinary business or social
contacts. Unless souls interact at a profound level, they can never
experience spiritual friendship. When you become friends
walking on the same path of Truth, you find a very powerful
bond exists between you.

If you are good at keeping an adequate psychological
distance from people, you will be able to get on with many
different types of people. However, in many cases, people
become too involved in their relationships or unable to create
friendships at all, so they miss the opportunity to learn from
others.

3. Beyond Good and Evil

If this world were of a monistic nature—in other words, if only
light existed, darkness being simply a lack of light, or if only
good existed, evil being the absence of good—there would be
no room to make a choice between "yes" or "no." It would be a
world in which there was no change, a standardized world that
would have to be accepted as it is. When you think in a monistic
way, all choice is removed and this greatly diminishes the possibility of education. If a dualistic perspective is taught, however, it
is possible to decide between good and bad, and as you continue
to make right choices, you can advance spiritually. If the world is

perceived in a monistic way, however, the efficacy of this type of education cannot be expected.

In fact, both from the point of view of the individual and of God, this world contains the duality of good and evil. As a result, we always have to undertake the task of discarding the evil and choosing the good. However, in the attempt to decide right from wrong, you should never forget the perspective of forgiveness, taking the passage of time into account. For instance, even if you encounter someone who seems evil, standing in your way and obstructing your efforts to pursue the Truth, you should instead consider that person not yet awakened. You must tell yourself that if they were to realize how things really are, they would not behave as they do, and that it is only because they have yet to discover the Truth that their eyes are covered with scales.

It can be said that this state of mind is akin to that of Jesus Christ when he was on the cross. He said, "Father, forgive them, for they do not know what they do" (Luke 23:34). These words show clearly that Jesus did not see things simply in terms of good and evil.

When talking about spiritual beings, we should not simply divide them into high spirits and low spirits. Rather, we can describe them as either developed or developing spirits. If you were to call a spirit a "lower spirit," it would naturally be angry, so you should rather consider it a "developing" spirit, a spirit that is going to develop sometime in the future, or a spirit that has temporarily stopped developing. If you regard them in this way, there is a chance that their characters will improve.

This becomes obvious when actually speaking to spirits from Hell. If you tell one that it is a bad spirit coming from Hell, it gets angry. However, if you say that although it is bad now, it has a good nature within, it will actually make an effort to improve. This may sound strange, but it is true. In this way, even when pointing out something to someone to be corrected, you should also try to offer praise, so as not to hurt the person's feelings.

4. Benefits and Drawbacks of Monism

There are many different arguments about monism and dualism. However, when we consider the reality of this world where human beings undergo spiritual training while living in a physical body, it has to be said that a monistic viewpoint of the world is misleading.

It is approximately one hundred million years since Hell came into existence, and these days, about half the people living on Earth fall to Hell after they die. Therefore, it is no use saying "originally there was no such thing as Hell or evil spirits, so they are not allowed to exist." This will not make them go away. It is much more sensible to accept this reality and try to work to improve the situation; it is pointless to try and keep the lid on the matter and forget it.

The monistic way of thinking says that only the light exists. But it is more accurate to say that at the source only light exists—if the light is blocked, naturally a shadow comes into existence. It is pointless to say that the shadow did not exist originally, because as long as there is something that cuts off the light, the shadow will form. To get rid of the shadow, it is necessary to remove the object that is obstructing the light. Accordingly, as long as we are undergoing spiritual training in this three-dimensional world on Earth, a dualistic view that accepts the existence of good and evil is correct, as this is the way things really are.

However, for the purpose of guiding those who are distressed toward the Light, the monistic theory has some relevance. The reason for this is that, when you are in the midst of fighting evil or your own worries, it is extremely difficult to escape. But, by focusing only on positive aspects, you may be able to break away from distressing circumstances. If you are tormenting yourself and your situation becomes painful, you can use the power of positive thinking to conquer the distress. If you are confronted by bad spirits, try to focus only on the positive side and determine to live with a constructive attitude. Then these spirits will leave you alone without any further struggle. The reason for this is that you will no longer emit the same vibrations as them.

It is the law that minds of the same wavelength attract each other; so if you are emitting bright, positive vibrations, these will repel the negative, destructive vibrations of bad spirits. Accordingly, an attitude of focusing on the positive side of the things and directing your mind toward the light is an extremely effective defense, and one that you can ill afford to ignore. If you examine your state of mind and realize that you spend a lot of your time thinking negative thoughts and focusing on the dark side, it would be a good idea for you to use the power of positive thinking.

Hell and its inhabitants do actually exist, so they must not be ignored. To be quite honest, at the present time it is very unlikely that everyone now living on Earth will return to Heaven after death, so it is necessary to inform people how harsh a life awaits them if they go to Hell.

5. Transcending Diversity

You may have learned about the diversity of values, and you may be capable of looking at things from a variety of angles, but if you think this is sufficient I am sorry to say that you are mistaken. Things are not that simple.

Let us say you decide to photograph Mount Fuji. You can take many pictures from different angles, but this is not to say that there is more than one Mount Fuji. There is of course only one mountain, but there are numerous ways in which it can be photographed. The view of Mount Fuji will vary according to where the picture is taken. Even if the pictures are all taken from the same place, they may differ depending on the season or weather. Similarly, what is essentially one can be expressed in numerous ways. I would like you to remember this when considering how to perceive the world.

If you think of things in terms of "good or evil," or of "yes or no," you may simply be trying to look at things as flat images projected on a single plane. However, when the same situation is seen from a higher dimension, the simple "yes or no" questions will no longer apply. For instance, Truth contains the teaching of justice that says that the righteous must be strong, and this may seem to contradict the teachings of love. If those two concepts are put on a single plane, there may be a contradiction. However, they can actually coexist within the vast multidimensional structure of the Laws of Truth.

A dice has six faces and, although each surface shows a different number, they are all parts of a single cube. A similar situation exists when talking about the Laws of Truth—when looked at from lower dimensions, the Laws appear diverse. However, it should be remembered that the different ways in which Truth is taught are the result of interpretations that conform to this world on Earth. Basically, these different ways all link together to create a single coherent whole.

If this is not understood, it will lead to the mistaken attitude of not attempting to overcome disagreements. Once you start thinking this way, you may easily be tempted to say, "human beings are free, so they can do whatever they like," and from there it is only a short step to Hell. Many of the inhabitants of Hell like to say, "I can use my freedom in whatever way I want and it is up to me what I make of it."

However, if a Buddhist says, "There are so many different values so why should I limit myself by bothering to take refuge in the Three Treasures?", this is a mistake. The willingness to accept a diversity of values helps you to forgive and tolerate those who have opinions different from your own. However, you should not use such willingness to justify yourself. When you have a difference of opinion with someone, you should not use the same logic to indulge yourself, saying the disagreement is a result of different ways of looking at things. If you continue to use diversity to your own advantage, there is a danger that you will move in a wrong direction away from the Truth, so you have to be careful.

IV. An Encounter with God

1. The Aspiration for Enlightenment

As I reflect on my childhood, I am always reminded just how much I was inclined to explore the Truth from my earliest days. The fact that there is an innate desire to search for the sublime within our souls is something we should all be thankful for. If you have a desire to reach for higher values, toward God, you should be grateful and remind yourself that you are both blessed and loved by Him.

If you have such an innate desire, it also means you aspire to enlightenment. Those who gather together in search of the Laws of Truth all share this longing, and so I would urge you never to forget to give thanks for being so blessed. There are a lot of people in this world who are unable to appreciate the infinite value of Truth. This can be likened to the way in which some people will admire a certain piece of music while others are unable to understand it. We are lucky to have been provided with ears that are capable of appreciating music. I sometimes wonder how animals hear music; although they may understand it to a certain extent, they probably can never appreciate it to the same degree as a human being. We can say that animals have not been provided with the same capacity for enjoyment as humans have. The same can be said of those who can appreciate the value of Truth and those who cannot.

2. Starting with Nothing

As I look back on my childhood, I am always reminded of the importance of the spirit of self-mastery. I have already spoken on this subject earlier in this book, and I think I can say that the ability to be master of myself is one of my strengths. I have never become complacent about the way I am, I have always sought to improve myself, and this is something that remains true of me to this day. You may feel, now or at different times, that your life leaves a lot to be desired when compared to your ideal, but the mere fact that you have a willingness to achieve your ideal some day provides you with the power to continue step by step until you reach that state. If you possess the spirit of self-mastery, then that alone is a great treasure, an essential quality that everyone needs to develop.

I am now president of the Institute for Research in Human Happiness and I teach the Laws of Truth to many. However, I myself started out in this world with nothing and it is only after several decades of spiritual discipline that I have reached this present stage. In five or ten years' time I will be somebody different and, in another twenty years, I will have undergone yet other changes. I have to undergo spiritual training just the same as anyone else.

No matter who we are, each and every one of us has to undergo spiritual training while we are on Earth. Among those who are now on Earth may be people who had previous lives as great figures, but the past is the past and the present is the present. When we come down to Earth, we all have to start with nothing, and how far you are able to progress depends upon the effort you make in spiritual discipline in this lifetime. It should also be remembered that as a result of your efforts and through various experiences, you are able to acquire a new personality. The character you develop is entirely up to you, it is something that you need to take responsibility for.

In my case, having come to live on Earth, I have developed the character with which I am now living. Even after I return to the other world, I will be able to express myself with this character and guide those on Earth. If you do not experience an earthly life living in a physical body, there is no way to develop your own character, and it is impossible to guide other people. You cannot name yourself because you have no name, you cannot show yourself because you have no form, you cannot exhibit your individuality because you have none. It is a very awkward situation to be in.

When we come to live on Earth, we can develop a very defined character. As a result of my current life on Earth, even after I return to the other world, I will be able to use the form of the individual named Ryuho Okawa to teach other spirits both in the spirit world and on Earth. This was one of the objectives of my current sojourn in this world.

3. Waiting for a Path to Open

Failures and disappointment are a part of life, and it can be said that it is these factors that make things so interesting. Each person has depths that others cannot really plumb, so there is always the possibility that your potential has not been fully exploited. This is true at the Institute of Research in Human Happiness, too. As its president, I am always concerned that I might not have done enough to help members develop their potentialities, or that there are people in this organization who may not have received the appreciation they deserve.

There is no need to think you are a failure just because people are unable to recognize or appreciate your abilities fully. Rather you should be thankful that there are some aspects of you that people do recognize. The same is true of promotion at a company. Some people advance rapidly while others do not; but this is not to say that those who do not receive promotion are not needed. In many cases their superiors want to help them, but find themselves unable to do so at a particular point in time, and worry that their employees may lose heart. If you find yourself in this position, you must not be oblivious to the feelings of those who are watching over you or turn your back on them. You must simply grit your teeth and wait for a path to success to open.

4. Controlling Inner Power

i) Softening the light

I myself experienced a lot of problems with personal relations. The amount of spiritual energy I have is inherently so large that my character is much more intense than might appear to be. It was once the case that, being so energetic, as soon as a thought occurred to me I would proceed to put it into action. As I devoted myself to self-improvement, I thought it only natural to put everything into my work. If I was not successful, I simply felt that it must have been because I was not trying hard enough and I redoubled my exertions.

Now I have learned the importance of controlling my inner energy and softening the light I emit. This has nothing to do with self-abasement or a superficial humility; it is the effort I make for the sake of love. If the light you emit is too bright, others will be unable to open their eyes and they will no longer be able to remain in your presence.

If you think only of yourself and become engrossed in strengthening your light, there is a danger that you will instigate rivalry in others and hurt their pride and dignity so you have to be careful. Here it is necessary to have the ability both to strengthen and weaken your inner light at will. The word energy could be used instead of light, and you must be able to exhibit both powerful and gentle energy as the situation demands, otherwise you will have difficulty getting along with others.

You may sometimes wish that others accepted the whole of you, just as you are, but this is like placing a big fish in front of people and asking them to eat it—they will not know where to start. Therefore, if you want people to accept you as you are, you should first "slice yourself up" to make yourself appear more appealing.

I would like you to understand that it is essential to be able to regulate the strength of the light you emit. One of the characteristics of young people is that, although they are capable of emitting a powerful light, they are unable to control it. They are so focused on radiating energy that they have not learned how to soften it. They will probably have to experience some setbacks before they master this art. However, before they are faced with these reversals, I would like to warn them that these problems arise because they emit too much light.

If you ever experience setbacks in relationships with others because of your inability to control your own light, there is no point in blaming those around you. Human beings all like to live in peace; if you disturb the harmony around you, then you must take responsibility. If a car speeds where it should not, it will crash; this is an obvious fact and also the reason we have speed limits. If you ignore the speed limit and press the accelerator to the floor just because your car can do two hundred kilometers per hour, then you will have to take responsibility for your actions. I sincerely hope, especially if you are young, that you will learn to control the strength of the energy you give out.

ii) *Changing yourself first*

A lot of people find it difficult to control their inward emotions and thinking. Control may be easier for those who are able to think logically, but most people find control very difficult and suffer as a result. If you have trouble coping with your own thinking and emotions, what chance do you have of coping with those of others, particularly people you do not like? You need to accept the fact that you cannot easily change others. Before you try to change them, you must first learn how to change yourself. Starting with small things, you should do your best to change yourself. As you continue in your efforts, one day you may be pleasantly surprised to find that the people around you are also beginning to change.

iii) *Fix a criterion upon which to base your thinking*

When you have trouble making up your mind about something, it is important for you to decide on some point that you will not change. In other words, you must adopt a particular yardstick against which you will measure the various factors. If you are incapable of creating a fixed point in this way, you will never be able to come to a decision.

For instance, if we were to decide on a criterion by which a person could qualify as a lecturer at the Institute for Research in Human Happiness, surely the first consideration would be whether that person would be a good guide for those who aspire to improve spiritually, not whether it would make the applicant happy. Seen in this light, you might ask if the candidate has sufficient knowledge of the Laws of Truth to carry out the task.

Consequently, you may come to the conclusion that the candidate needs to study a little more before becoming a lecturer.

As you can see from this example, when you have trouble making up your mind, you should find one constant factor upon which you can base your thinking. Once you have decided to use this factor as the pivot, you must continue organizing your thoughts around it. When your thoughts will not settle, you must find a single immutable point that you cannot afford to ignore and use this as the base. Then you will find a course you can follow. Of course, there will be some factors that need to be cast aside, and, this being so, you must make an effort to do this. You have to be logical and consistent. If you continue to do this work, you will gradually obtain more control over your inner states.

5. Acquiring a New Viewpoint

In my twenties, when I worked as an employee of a Japanese trading company, I spent approximately one year living in the United States. This stay was a very fruitful experience, particularly because I went as an adult with a reasonable knowledge of the world and some business experience, not as a student. It actually turned out to be the experience of a lifetime.

The most important lesson I learned through living abroad was that, by changing my perspective, I was able to see things in a different light. The information that we acquire through our education and surroundings can often be biased, but if we are able to look at it from a totally different angle, we are able to see where the source of a misunderstanding lies. After I had observed Japan from the United States, I returned to Japan and then observed the United States from a Japanese perspective. Having had this experience, I am aware that somebody who can see both sides of the argument has quite different views to somebody who only knows one side. Seeing both sides allows you to understand what the situation really is.

In order to grasp a truth in all its forms, it is necessary for us to undergo a variety of experiences. Let me take the example of Mount Fuji again. Mount Fuji is generally perceived as a cone-shaped mountain, but, in actual fact, when seen from one particular angle, there is a part protruding from the right-hand slopes which cannot be seen when the mountain is viewed from other angles. Similarly, unless you look at a thing or a situation from a variety of perspectives you will not be able to grasp its true form. When a map is made, the technique of triangulation is used, and, in the same way, before you are able to grasp the truth, you will have to take into account a variety of factors.

I always teach the importance of self-reflection. The Eight-fold Path is an essential yardstick against which you need to measure yourself to find the True Self. However, on the other hand, once you have gone through many experiences and realized that there are many different ways of thinking, things that had appeared to be major obstacles in the past turn out to be in fact quite minor. Because new knowledge and experience will help you discover new aspects of yourself, they are worth their weight in gold. With regard to knowledge, you should make the effort to study subjects you have previously ignored or had no interest in before. By doing this, you will be able to acquire new perspectives that will lead you in new directions. When it comes to experience, you should not allow yourself to be bound by habit, but break out and try doing things that would have been quite outside the scope of your interests before. For instance, if you do not just limit yourself to your usual circle of friends but sometimes meet different kinds of people, you will be exposed to a completely new way of looking at things.

V. Increasing the Value of Time

Time can be divided into "relative time" and "absolute time"—both these different types of time actually do exist. One day is made up of twenty-four hours and there is nothing that can be done to lengthen or shorten this physically. However, it is possible to increase the amount of time we spend improving our souls. I would call this "absolute time." "Relative time," in contrast, is time as measured by a clock. It is the kind of time that Karl Marx referred to in his Labor Theory of Value as a commodity that can be sold like any other commodity at a price determined by the time of the labor necessary to produce it. In the future, however, I feel that this theory will be clearly rejected.

One hour as measured by the clock (relative time) is the same for every single person, but the value it carries, absolute time, varies from person to person. For instance, if several people listen to a one-hour lecture, they will all be there for the same period of time, but some of them will create an idea based on what they heard in the lecture that is much more valuable than anything the others do. The differences in the worth of the thought they hold during and after the lecture will result in a difference in the worth of the hour they spent. If they slept through the entire speech, then the time they spent will have been of no value at all. But one person may find a clue or the seed of an idea that will enable them to live a better life in future. If the idea is developed, and prosperity becomes a reality, this means that value has been created. From this, you can see that the same hour is not always of equal value.

I hope that you will all make every effort to increase the value of every hour you spend. The way to do this is to ask yourself questions such as, "How can I use this one hour for the greatest benefit of my soul?" or "How can I use the spare time I have in the afternoon to get the most out of it for the sake of my spiritual improvement?"

Exactly the same applies to me. I am always thinking of how to use my time to be of greater benefit to more people. It is not easy, but I always try to make the best choice. I invest my time to make it of the greatest use to the greatest number of people. It is upon this criterion that I base all my thinking.

Living your life to the full in this way can actually have the same effect as having a longer life. Although the physical time you live in this world may not change, it is possible to increase the value you produce, using your time more effectively.

VI. Rising to an Extraordinary Level of Love

1. Opening the Door to the Subconscious

At the beginning of this book, I wrote of my experiences when I came into contact with the spirit world, and explained that before this happened I had undergone a period of introspection. If some being that claims to be "God" appears to you all of a sudden, you should be on your guard. Actually, before you can contact the spirit world, you have to experience an introspective period. You may have a strong desire to set aside time to look within yourself, in silence. As you continue to do this daily, you may at some time find that the door to your subconscious is gradually beginning to open.

This applies to everyone; there are no exceptions to this rule. It is necessary to sit quietly and look deeply within yourself. This is how preparations are made for the soul to open the door to the world of the subconscious. This means that people who are always busy, rushing about in a panic trying to keep up with their work, will never be able to gain access to their subconscious. There may be cases in which these sorts of people think they are successful, but in actual fact what has happened is that they have suddenly begun to experience unusual sensations due to questionable spirits that have approached them.

2. Crystallizing Your Thoughts

What I teach at IRH consists of a wide range of philosophies, and many of them have been formed around the core concepts I discovered during my earlier studies. As I continued deep contemplation on such seed thoughts, my own philosophy gradually took shape and matured. For example, as I mentioned at the beginning of this book, I spent a lot of time reflecting on the phrase "Love, Nurture, and Forgive" which came to me as a spiritual revelation, and as a result, my philosophy on the stages of love was created.

Just as ice or snow needs a core around which to crystallize, so do thoughts. You need to search for a core philosophy, or adopt one from somebody else, around which you can strive to crystallize your thoughts. If you continue to make this effort, your thoughts will begin to take shape and you will form your own philosophy.

Therefore, it is important that you first find a seed thought and then take the time to consider it very carefully. After you have reflected on it for six months, a year, or perhaps two or three, it will gradually begin to blossom and become your very own philosophy. If you are in a room full of people and somebody asks you to explain your personal philosophy, I would like you to be one of those who can stand up and talk for an hour or two, or even three. You do not want to be one of those people who has nothing to say, with no opinions on anything; rather, you should make the effort to create your own philosophy.

As you make an effort to learn different lessons and have a wide range of experiences, these will all build up around the kernel of thought you have planted within yourself and crystallize into a single coherent form. If you create and store a number of these crystals, adding to them as you get the chance, you will gradually grow into a person who is capable of leading others.

To have your own philosophy is very important, and whether or not you have developed this will determine the realm you go to after death. People who think about nothing day in, day out, will only be capable of reacting to their environment through conditioned responses when they arrive in the other world. On the other hand, those who have developed the habit of thinking deeply will be able to live a much richer life there.

In the world we go to after death, thought is everything, and so it is important that you develop the inner world of thoughts within you while you are still on Earth. This will allow you to expand the scope of your activity in the next world, so I would like you to expand your inner world through thinking in as far-reaching a way as possible while you are alive. It is much more important than expanding your range of activities only to seek pleasure in this world.

3. Confrontation with Evil Spirits

Finally, I would like to talk about confrontations with malicious spirits. Some people may gain the access to their subconscious and one day make contact with the inhabitants of the spirit world. I would like to warn you that if this happens to you, you will be exposed to great risk, so please be on your guard.

When you are living an ordinary life in this earthly world and are not in contact with the spirit world, influences from the other world are limited. Even if you have momentary doubts or worries, these do not cause much trouble. However, once you establish a connection with the spirit world, having negative thoughts means you are directly exposed to a world of negativity, in accordance with the law that same wavelengths attract each other. This is true for everybody; it is said that "one thought leads to three thousand worlds" and, sure enough, your thoughts can take you to all sorts of realms in the spirit world.

As you can see from this, gaining spiritual abilities does not ensure you will always be connected to the heavenly world. Consequently, unless you are capable of maintaining inner peace and harmony, you will be in real danger. To keep your heart and mind always attuned to the heavenly realm, it is important you get rid of worldly attachments. The discipline of eliminating attachment to worldly desires is taught not because it is desirable from a moralistic point of view; rather, it should be undertaken because once you have learned to open your subconscious, any attachment you may still possess will put you in great peril. Malicious spirits ask for only the smallest opportunity to enter your inner world. I want you to realize just how dangerous this is. Even if you are an Angel of Light, you are not exempt. Unless you make efforts to progress with steady steps, always looking back to your starting point, you are in great danger.

Evil spirits are really ferocious. The higher your position, the more important your job, the more likely you are to become a target. They will purposely aim to bring you down and, if you are conceited and think you are more important than anyone else, there is no way to save you. Even angels are incapable of defending themselves alone, without the help of higher spirits, once the devils have decided to bring them down. So it is vital that you have friends, friends with whom you are connected through faith. In addition, if you have faith, this will serve as a direct connection to God. This means that the evil spirits will not be able to attack you as a mortal human being, they will have to fight God Himself.

For this reason, evil spirits will take every opportunity to try and destroy your faith. They will sow doubts in your mind, cause confusion to your sense of what is advantageous and disadvantageous, and whisper honeyed words in your ear. For instance, they will tell you that you are being treated unfairly, that really you should have a much higher position but you have been cheated out of what is your due by others. In these sorts of ways, they will try to destroy your faith. If they ever achieve this aim, you will find yourself alone, and unfortunately there will be little chance of victory over them. Confrontation with evil spirits is an issue that has persisted throughout history, but it is absolutely essential to find ways of overcoming them.

To achieve this, it is most important that you become free of any major concerns. If you feel that you have allowed yourself to become fixated on something in particular, then you should make an effort to direct your attention to something else, to become relaxed and filled with peace. It is important that you develop a frank disposition and become as free as possible from concerns, for this will be a great strength that you can rely on when confronting evil spirits.

Another theory you can use if you feel yourself under attack by malicious spirits is one that I myself have used. Having established a contact with the spirit world, if you ever come to experience strange phenomena and feel you are under attack from the dark realms, day and night, you should try getting rid of any interest in the other world. You must then take a new look at yourself as a human being, as you really are, as an ordinary citizen, then aim to rebuild yourself. You must make an effort to become a person that others will recognize to be "good."

When evil spirits first begin to affect you, you are no longer able to understand the difference between right and wrong. If this happens, you must examine yourself as an ordinary citizen, to see whether you are somebody that people like to be with, somebody whose mere presence is seen as a blessing. This is your final check as an individual, and if you are this sort of person you will be protected from evil. You should cease all interests in spiritual matters and spiritual phenomena at once, and live your life simply as yourself. You must try to develop yourself to be somebody who makes others happy, and practice the love that gives. If you think that you are special, evil will use this to find its way into your inner world, so you must be careful to banish all such thoughts from your mind.

If you can put the simple maxim, "Love, Nurture, and Forgive," into practice, you will succeed in transforming your life. You will find you have taken a great step toward a richer life.

What Is IRH?

The Institute for Research in Human Happiness (IRH) is an organization of people who aim to cultivate their souls and deepen their wisdom. The teachings of IRH are based on the spirit of Buddhism. The two main pillars are the attainment of spiritual wisdom and the practice of "love that gives."

Keep updated with
IRH MONTHLY

featuring a lecture by Ryuho Okawa. Each volume also includes a question-and-answer session with Ryuho Okawa on real life problems.

For more information, please contact local offices of IRH.

Also available
MEDITATION RETREATS

Educational opportunities are provided to people who wish to seek the path of Truth. The Institute organizes meditation retreats for English speakers in Japan and other countries.

THE INSTITUTE FOR RESEARCH IN HUMAN HAPPINESS
Kofuku-no-Kagaku

Tokyo
1-2-38 Higashi Gotanda
Shinagawa-ku
Tokyo 141-0022
Japan
Tel: 81-3-5793-1729
Fax: 81-3-5793-1739
Email: JDA02377@nifty.com
www.irhpress.co.jp

New York
2nd Fl. Oak Tree Center
2024 Center Avenue
Fort Lee, NJ 07024
U.S.A.
Tel: 1-201-461-7715
Fax: 1-201-461-7278

Los Angeles
Suite 104
3848 Carson Street
Torrance, CA 90503
U.S.A.
Tel: 1-310-543-9887
Fax: 1-310-543-9447

San Francisco
1291 5th Ave.
Belmont, CA 94002
U.S.A.
Tel / Fax: 1-650-802-9873

Hawaii
419 South St. #101
Honolulu, HI 96813
U.S.A.
Tel: 1-808-587-7731
Fax: 1-808-587-7730

Toronto
484 Ravineview Way
Oakville, Ontario L6H 6S8
Canada
Tel / Fax: 1-905-257-3677

London
65 Wentworth Avenue
Finchley, London N3 1YN
United Kingdom
Tel : 44-20-8346-4753
Fax: 44-20-8343-4933

Sao Paulo
(Ciencia da Felicidade do
Brasil)
Rua Gandavo
363 Vila Mariana
Sao Paulo, CEP 04023-001
Brazil
Tel: 55-11-5574-0054
Fax: 55-11-5574-8164

Seoul
178-6 Songbuk-Dong
Songbuk-ku, Seoul
Korea
Tel: 82-2-762-1384
Fax: 82-2-762-4438

Melbourne
P.O.Box 429 Elsternwick
VIC 3185
Australia
Tel / Fax: 61-3-9503-0170

ABOUT THE AUTHOR

Ryuho Okawa, founder and spiritual leader of the Institute for Research in Human Happiness (IRH), has devoted his life to the exploration of the spirit world and ways to human happiness.

He was born in 1956 in Tokushima, Japan. After graduating from the University of Tokyo, he joined a major Tokyo based trading house and studied international finance at the City University of New York. In 1986, he renounced his business career and established IRH.

He has been designing IRH spiritual workshops for people from all walks of life, from teenagers to business executives. He is known for his wisdom, compassion and commitment to educating people to think and act in spiritual and religious ways.

The members of IRH follow the path he teaches, ministering to people who need help by spreading his teachings.

He is the author of many books and periodicals, including *The Laws of the Sun*, *The Golden Laws*, *The Laws of Eternity*, and *The Starting Point of Happiness*. He has also produced successful feature length films (including animations) based on his works.